Odes of St. Hemisphere

Double Movement Publications

ISBN: 978-1-312-02197-6

Cover Illustration: *Forget-Me Relents,* 2014, oil and graphite on paper.

Double Movement Publications
2239 SE 47th Avenue
Portland, Oregon, 97215

for John and Geoffrey

Odes of St. Hemisphere

You and I were in the middle of some kind of
discussion about perspective or something a lot
like perspective. You remember I was called away
to deal with a family issue. That turned out to
be a test. A decoy. A piece of paper shaped like
the sort of thing one might use to write a poem.

In the
fact a
tissue
self a
carded
timber

I was involved in this perspective, a kind of
family or decoy, where the middle ground was
taken up by local merchants, their cries for
attention, the soiled shine of various wares. A
young bearded man bought a wooden pole to use as
a walking staff. At another stall, flowers fell
about like a fountain of red, yellow flesh. I was
not over-committed or determined to make this my
place. I was not ready to sign off. I was like a
videographer who keeps putting the camera away,
taking it up, putting it down. Who cannot click
<send>.

intransient
non transit
inequitable

flower that
fell shower
of a flower

in contests
beauties if
that beauty

So, the introduction. How we came to be. And being, how we became. How we, and the nature of being, having become, became the We that we diagnose as being. That, and this matter of tickets for passage. I will not over-extend your attention. I give over Maybe for the purer stuff of What.

A kind of professor is standing by who knows family and related reconciliations.

This being said, I am in a red, red room. It's actually red and not at all distracting. Do you think? That was the easiest part of the entire business.

A recipe, or article:

a cheese
a fork
a sandwich

The more we speak the greater the likelihood of, precisely, What. In the same way, this work is too much a Knowing, but that is its place, if not its point. Not precisely. Allusive. Little river, little thought. Running, bouncing, exuding and detracting. Christmas parties. Audio events. Almost everyone agreed that time of matters. We cannot pretend to be ashamed in ways that stack one on the other, like playing cards, or mattresses for sale. We cannot be kept.

---

sense from
fact sense
this float
terrible a
floating I
green with
this sense

john met barbara who knew joel from work. joel
knew john from stories a roommate told him.
barbara and steve went away weekends to one or
another town on the ocean. john hadn't been to
see the ocean in almost two years. the roommate's
name was tom, tom miller. a shot rang out.

joel and barbara were close to a thing which
would never get any closer unless you count that
it might seem important some time later. john and
steve had several things in common on paper. we
carried the canoes over some wooded terrain then
back to the river and continued on our journey.

It took us this long - this long! - to get to our
novel.

Our novel -

When I look over my life I look over the past
three or four days. That is about all I can hold
in my mind's eye. If I say, Let's observe the
bigger picture, I surrender focus. Not that any
past few days offer much focus.

I believe that good writing offers a slice of
life that any reader can apply to their own
novel.

Every time I do this I have a different set of
occurrences, so I am not confused, but I am at
sea. I do not know if others feel the same way. I
have observances and standards for personal
conduct. When I am awake, I am not asleep. Even
my sleep falls under the purview of the observed
and tallied. That sounds rather more strict than
is true. Oh, I yearn for freedom. To flip about
the crags of life like the veritable mountain
goat. But I transgress.

A thread passing through a needle, a needle
dropped for other chores and forgotten. It is
disturbing, what does not appear to fall to
disuse. Tyranny and the money principle.
Electronic books. Sex as, What I want.

Is there anything new? Well, it is all new. That
is the weariness and the prompt: to capitulate
(which is never capitulation) and say, Enough.
Enough of what. See, we are perfectly alone.

small faces in a big world, but
a world not so big it turns out

lipstick green
a car so blue
occasionally
I think about you

tattered clothes
a closet neat
forgive the man
his crooked feet

the wind alive
it weeps and cries
alive at pigeons, dope,
mannequins, ties

the work, the work
I feel like a jerk
a bent fork or
bankrupt donor

one in a while
depending on my mood
I think of you
I feel my blood

Oh the day was bright
the sun was steady
examples lay about
like crumpled teddies

_____

I was president.
A flower.
A pipsqueak charm.
A colony tower.

Beads and charms
charms and beads
I like po-ems
no one reads

I was thinking of the charm of objects, bordering
on people as charms, when the lights went out.
Jeremy grabbed a candlestick. The rest of us
followed at a respectful distance. We gained the
outside, where the curtain of night seemed fallen
in a heap to reveal what lies behind the night.
That one night only? I could not know then, but I
know now. Jennifer, that was her name, yes,
grabbed my hand. My heart had gone all stiff. I
seemed to know the torture of the clattering
engine. We played music. At dawn, dawn. Perhaps
the parents of now-forgotten friends crossed
Failinghouse Square on the way to their jobs.
Work. That was still a strange pre-determinedly
outworn notion. But I was young and foolish then.
I was wise in the ways of youth and blind to
colloquies. I don't even know what that means. A
kite sails over the sea. A paper cup pitched.
Promise met tomorrow and settled in for a long
talk. I was not present for the negotiations
that, all things considered, were a success.
Smiles, cheers. Jen wears gray, even her heels,
and still looks good.

Oh, Jen. Imagine if we were the clothes we wear.
If only.

Writing as if we are starting again will not do,
nor as if we are ending anything. It being
understood we are not correcting or correct.
Writing that is writing will not do, that is not
writing should have thumb to wrist pulse.
Poetries that borrow tableware are fine indeed. I
can't keep track of everything I think or feel. A
woman writing who falls for every bloody sunset
but will not be dictated to. Whom one cannot
dictate to. Who, dictator, will do. Woman like
trees and trees unlike women. The word Woman, the
mention of trees. Writing as if capitulating or
canvassing, catapulting, all these like fresh
vegetables for sale, all in a line, in wooden
crates that may have served another purpose. The
draft animal, the decommissioned howitzer.

I like a truck, the drives, like how cold rivers
make me feel inside. Inside here, where poems
sprout like hats falling from a shelf in a closet
dark.

Someone said a little thing.
Someone said a big thing.

Dead leaves fell about the blushing bride like
fish on the deck of a Russian trawler.

Am I alone?
Am I alone, at last?

Newspapers pass back and forth when the wind says
I am alone like a solitary Ruby in the crown of a
virgin princess.

Cause is not the primary determinant in an
inverse equation (language) where utterance
declares its precincts.

Like a special day.
Lavender-scented bellhops. Periodic songs.

A woman touched a shoulder, the man having lost
all kinds of time getting coffee, going through
his messages, getting ready for the day.

What is time?

A kind of stiff, off-white cloth, drawn over
things whose shape is obscured, sure, but all you
have to do is take off the fucking cloth.

We will not be popular today.
We were not popular yesterday, and we will not be
popular today.

A flock of birds passed over the land of
interest. It was late morning, and we had only
just stepped into the day.

A kind of torch passed over the the land. A torch
ablaze, that gave no heat.

The straps of the backpack bit into my shoulders
as they had the day before. I was tired of
thinking, that great democracy.

The flower of error sprang before me. I did not
own time, I thought. I own nothing that is mine.

The clouds fell to the earth like the pennies in
a parlor trick. A man stepped forward with a pan
of steaming dumplings. They smelled delicious.

A suite of poems for the city
bus blue as starlight bussing
busables or bussed as bussing

speech or conversation I said
conversation all mentionables
even dot-dash-got the control

middle-aged he whose poetical
backsounds drift into a legal
email says too much fun I say

misery attracts; pleasantness
chases the world into corners
where, other gentles ruminate

maybe typing, the act, is sex
in some unnamed realm & coins
into a jukebox and fresh beer

@ sum pnt the thoughts became
words on the hook the vig ten
points over living room temps

dash-dash-dash. St Hemisphere
rolled to one side & released
a billowfart of gray feathers

worrying, warying.

I am a kind of worn eye untroubling facts with
precision. So martha and bernadette found an
apartment.

Up to this point best practices suggested writing
at this moment. As to the work implied by the
title "poet" I had fallen off the shelf and into
a kind of gentle, pillowing combine. I, the bale.
You, a coy ingenue. Time, the road-bound
tax collector.

To be clear the ingenue is a lawyer or record
producer having assumed pastoral forms by virtue
of the fleeting but no less perfect concretions
of one's mind stet in place of one's mind
concerned (another approximation) or devoted to
worry.

Worry, the great one.

I will die, a president elected, and the lights
in the Plaid Pantry will go on.

You were alone in Eden. When no one came, you
made yourself quiet and, by sheer luck, woke into
contemporary sleep.

Ding!

day that is new
day that is old
day that is new
night loosening

We need to get organized. The parties will be
here, to the right and left while wheeling about
- at this point, now. And now. Jen, you will come
around over my right shoulder with the number 2
spot. Bob, train No. 1 steady on the party
downwind from No. 2. There. Are we clear on the
sequence? Good. Now, we have a guy handling the
music and you all have your cues. Soon as the
dust settles I'll go out, say a few words, and
dish off the hardware. Let's pick up and go over
it again from daybreak.

The actress -
the Hollywood
A clandestine
signing sighs

I was at work
a trombone of
leonine flesh
paint conceit

almost type &
just hit that
button, these
citizen dials

not that much
not canvassed
neighborhoods
& percentages

flesh a glass
or was a song
stop. people.
& the film...

_____

I can see that we are connected, but this is not
the sort of thing a gentleman brags about. A
gentleman is considerate, sharing where it might
do some good, and careful to show, artfully, that
some things are to remain hidden.

A gentleman is like a cathedral, the flying
buttresses, under a dark and gloomy night. This
too is the French language.

We saw a movie featuring reels of film, a period
movie with a point, the fleeting exactness of
love.

I rolled over and slept as long as I could, the
French countryside receding and approaching with
the rhythm of a dray pulling a wagon full of hay.

In small ways, a fire, one you can stamp out and
not be surprised when it rekindles. A fire
composed of little, fleeting flames. Some blue,
some yellow.

The cloak she threw over her arm, to go walking
in the same garden I was accustomed to visit in
the middle of the day.

Time is one chair among other chairs.

Non-convertible
Non-converting,
the slip - blue
aluminum sonnet

O poetry. You &
warm bedtimes -
you & celery or
me & you & time

I came upon the
faceting tiger,
I launched upon
its spiral back

Decades and the
leap, family or
work so the day
of the decision

I guess, or was
it the tiger? I
am a poor pupil
of the occurred

bt I was saying
you, & you were
offshore waving
the cargo over.

The gentleman is concerned.

Look at his face.

He is fully awake, perhaps not well-rested, no,
but reasonably alert and fully capable. And yet
he leaves work early, day after day, and once or
twice a week, he goes to a local bar to write
poetry.

He is not angry, the gentleman, nor impotent. He
is well fed, but fit. There is no sign of cancer
that we are aware of.

On the top of a mountain, a flag. And a closer
look reveals that the mountain is a kind of
sculpture made from steel and glass, the kind of
materials one sees in office buildings.

The gentleman is not a pioneer.

Perhaps he thinks too much, or too little. Who
can say.

There are pursuits, attentions. The bottom of his
glass predicts a second beer, perhaps a third.
That's enough, I think.

I think I am done, said the gentleman.

_____

This is the earth
This is our world
This is the sense
- a sense of tone

just like a stick
of yellow pigment
dried and wrapped
among others, too

I am of the crowd
How much to be sd
with no research?
let's play it out

a body of work as
a clump of autumn
leaves the cities
manage to control

a bit of ribbon a
sweatshirt factor
the colors bright
or/in combination

elevator talk, my
chorus. driving a
nail that doesn't
drive & so Spring

Women. Sympathy -
Peoples. Sympathy
- circular sounds
money at the gate

blood is a regret
if sound held the
hand But first my
name then my life

The president of circumstance is not, is not a
gentleman. He is not willing to concede, having
developed to the point of poster bombs context as
his mate and his emolument. The forest canopy
lets loose scattered, artful cries. At the edge
of the village, fishermen pick distractedly at
their nets. Clouds roll in like hay bales
tumbling off the gate of a pickup truck, the
winter a long one, and beef needing our help.

Help them, help them to the gate, the heated
interior, the hissing valves and last bright
light.

Everything surrounds a president. Nothing happens
in the center of a whirlwind. That is the secret
of nothing.

For every day, a bead on a necklace. Two beads
for Christmas.

I call this a date, this sliding of locked wheels
to a skidding stop. Stop. It sounds like a rhyme
for a kind of jungle flower.

There, near the protruding foot of St.
Hemisphere.

www.ingramcontent.com/pod-product-compliance
Lightning Source LLC
Chambersburg PA
CBHW031336040426
42443CB00005B/368